WE ARE BORN TO BE REAL ; NOT TO BE PERFECT

EMBRACING AUTHENTICITY AND IMPERFECTION IN THE WORLD OF EXPECTATIONS

ARCHIT PATIL

Made with ♥ on the Notion Press Platform
www.notionpress.com

"Dedicated to all those who have ever felt the **weight of perfectionism,** who have been conditioned to believe that they need to be flawless, and who have struggled to meet the unrealistic expectations of others.

To those who have been told to hide their scars, to conceal their struggles, and to present a perfect facade to the world. May this book be a reminder that your worth is not measured by your flaws, but by your courage to be yourself.

May you find the freedom to **embrace your quirks,to love your scars**, and **to live a life thatisunapologetically real**. May you discover that your imperfections are not weaknesses, but strengths that make you unique and beautiful.

To those who have supported me on this journey, thank you for your unwavering belief in my message. Your encouragement, guidance, and love have meant the world to me.

And to those who will read these words, I hope they inspire you to break free from the chains of perfection and to discover the beauty of being real. May you find solace in knowing that you are not alone, that your struggles are valid, and that your authenticity is the greatest gift you can offer the world.

May this book be a beacon of hope, a reminder that you are enough, and that your realness is the most precious thing you can offer. May you be brave, may you be kind"

Contents

Preface

I still remember the day I realized that I was tired of pretending. Tired of putting on a mask of perfection, tired of hiding my imperfections, and tired of trying to be someone I'm not. It was exhausting, and it was suffocating me.

As I looked around, I saw that I wasn't alone. Everyone was pretending, everyone was hiding, and everyone was struggling to keep up the act. We were all trying to be perfect, but at what cost?

I realized that I had a choice to make. I could continue down the path of perfectionism, or I could take a step back and embrace my imperfections. I could be real.

It wasn't easy, let me tell you. It took courage, vulnerability, and a willingness to take risks. But as I started to peel off the layers of pretension, I discovered a sense of freedom and authenticity that I had never known before.

That's when I knew that I had to share this message with others. I had to let people know that they don't have to be perfect, that they can be real, and that their imperfections are what make them beautiful.

This book is my journey, but it's also yours. It's a journey of self-discovery, of embracing our imperfections, and of finding the courage to be ourselves. It's not always easy, but it's worth it.

Through these pages, I share my story, my struggles, and my triumphs. I share practical strategies for cultivating self-acceptance, self-compassion, and self-love. And I invite you to join me on this journey of liberation.

We are born to be real, not to be perfect. Let us embrace our imperfections, let us celebrate our uniqueness, and let us find the courage to be ourselves.

This book is for anyone who has ever felt like they don't measure up, anyone who has ever felt like they need to hide, and anyone who has ever felt like they're not enough. It's for anyone who is tired of pretending and ready to be real.

Let's take this journey together. Let's be real, let's be vulnerable, and let's be free.

Don't just find the meaning of meaningless world !!!

PREFACE

Foreword

Welcome to a journey of liberation! In the following pages, Archit Patil (AUTHOR) shares a powerful message that has the potential to transform your life. With vulnerability, honesty, and insight, he invites you to reexamine the pressures that have led you to hide behind masks of perfection.

For too long, we have been conditioned to believe that perfection is the ultimate goal. We strive for flawless skin, perfect grades, and impeccable behavior. We curate our social media profiles to present a highlight reel of our lives, hiding our imperfections and struggles. But in doing so, we sacrifice our authenticity, our creativity, and our humanity.

The pursuit of perfection is a myth, a myth that has led us down a path of disconnection, anxiety, and burnout. We compare ourselves to others, feeling inadequate and insecure. We fear failure, so we play it safe, stifling our innovation and progress. We hide our true selves, afraid of judgment and rejection.

But what if we told you that there is another way? What if you could break free from the shackles of perfectionism and embrace your true self? What if you could find the courage to be imperfect, to take risks, and to be vulnerable?

This book is a call to arms, a summons to reclaim your authenticity, and to find the courage to be yourself. Archit Patil shares his own journey of self-discovery, and invites you to join him on this path of radical self-acceptance.

Through these pages, you will discover:

- The myth of perfection and how it has held you back
- The power of vulnerability and imperfection

• Practical strategies to cultivate self-acceptance and self-compassion
• Inspiring stories of people who have embraced their authenticity and found freedom

You will learn that imperfection is not something to be ashamed of, but something to be celebrated. You will discover that your worth is not measured by your achievements, but by your willingness to be yourself. You will find that the most powerful thing you can be is not perfect, but real.

This book is not a quick fix or a magic solution. **It is a journey, a journey that requires courage, patience,and kindness**. But the reward is worth it: a life that is authentic, raw, and truly fulfilling.

So take a deep breath, let your guard down, and allow yourself to be present. Allow yourself to feel, to think, and to be. We are born to be real, not to be perfect. Let this book be your guide on the journey towards radical self-acceptance, and towards a life that is truly yours.

As you read these words, remember that you are not alone. You are part of a community of people who are tired of pretending, tired of hiding, and tired of being perfect. You are part of a movement that values authenticity, imperfection, and vulnerability.

Let us rise up and embrace our true selves. Let us shatter the myth of perfection and find the beauty in our imperfections.

Acknowledgements

Like all Books ,

WE ARE BORN TO BE REAL NOT TO BE PERFECT wouldn't have been possible without the help of countless people whose insight , guidance had helped me through out my life , There are to many to list them all , but a few who have particularly assistive :

VAISHALI PATIL (AUTHOR'S MOM) : Guided entirely in my life along with it ,herpersective , recomendations are engraved in few chapters.

KRISHNA PATIL ,SANJEEVANI PATIL (AUTHOR'S GRANDFATHER & GRANDMOTHER): Motivated in all sorts of life , There teachings are present in some chapters.

There are many people Sahil (**my brother**), **Ramkrishna(my dad) ,some well wishers, Nishkarsh,Anushka,Tejasvi,Shravya,Aalandi,Mugdha, Bhavika,Savari,Aaliya(my best friends) and my erudite teachers**

THANK YOU :) FOR YOUR BENEVOLENT ASSISTANCE !!

Prologue

"*Embracing Authenticity*"

In a world where flawless facades and polished personas reign supreme, it's easy to forget that our true beauty lies in our imperfections. We're constantly bombarded with messages telling us to strive for perfection – to conform, to conform, to conceal our true selves. But what if I told you that this pursuit of perfection is not only futile but also suffocating?

From a young age, we're conditioned to believe that perfection is the ultimate goal. We're taught to hide our flaws, to mask our vulnerabilities and to present a curated version of ourselves to the world. But this relentless quest for perfection comes at a steep price. We sacrifice our individuality, our creativity and our capacity for genuine connection.

What if, instead of striving for an unattainable ideal, we embraced our authentic selves? What if we celebrated our quirks, our flaws and our unique experiences? Imagine living in a world where vulnerability is valued, where imperfections are beautiful and where being real is the ultimate strength.

This book is an invitation to break free from the shackles of perfectionism and to discover the liberating power of authenticity. It's a journey of self-discovery, self-acceptance and self-love. Through personal stories, practical wisdom and inspiring insights, we'll explore what it means to be truly real.

We'll delve into the masks we wear, the fears that hold us back and the courage it takes to be vulnerable. We'll examine the toxic culture of comparison and the freedom found in embracing our uniqueness. And we'll uncover the transformative power of self-compassion, self-forgiveness and self-expression.

Join me on this journey as we challenge the status quo and redefine what it means to be perfect. Let's shatter the illusion of flawlessness and find beauty in our imperfections. Let's uncover the strength in vulnerability and the wisdom in embracing our true selves.

In the following pages, you'll find stories of struggle, resilience and triumph. You'll encounter voices that echo your own doubts, fears and hopes. And you'll discover practical guidance to help you release the weight of perfectionism and step into the freedom of being real.

So, take a deep breath, let your guard down and join the movement. Let's celebrate our imperfections, our individuality and our shared humanity. We are born to be real, not to be perfect. It's time to embrace our true selves and **live a life that's authentic**, wholehearted and uniquely our own.

CHAPTER ONE

THE MASK OF PERFECTION

The Mask of Perfection

The pressure to conform to societal standards is overwhelming. **From a young age, we're told to be perfect**, to look perfect, to act perfect. We're bombarded with messages from media, social media, and even our own families, telling us that we need to be more, do more, achieve more. But what's the cost?

Perfectionism is a heavy burden to carry. It's the constant feeling of never being good enough, never measuring up. It's the voice in our heads that says we need to be more, do more, achieve more. It's the relentless pursuit of an unattainable ideal. But perfection is a myth. It's an unattainable goal that we can never reach. And yet, we strive for it, often at the expense of our own well-being.

The mask of perfection is a clever disguise. **It hides our true selves,our imperfections, our quirks, and our flaws**. It presents a false narrative, one that says we have it all together, that we're perfect. But the truth is, we're not perfect. We're human. We make mistakes. We have flaws. And that's okay.

I remember struggling with perfectionism myself. I would spend hours on a single task, trying to get it just right. I would beat myself up over tiny mistakes and dwell on them for days. I would compare myself to others, feeling like I wasn't good enough. But one day, I realized that this wasn't living. This was just existing. And I knew I had to make a change.

The impact of perfectionism on our mental health and relationships cannot be overstated. It leads to anxiety, depression, burnout, and isolation. It causes us to push away those who care about us, because we're too afraid to let them see our imperfections. But it's time to break free from this myth.

Let's start by acknowledging the ways in which we've felt pressured to conform to societal standards. Have you ever felt like you need to look a certain way, act a certain way, or achieve certain things to be accepted? Have you ever felt like you're not good enough, like you're just pretending to be someone you're not?

Now, let's explore the impact of perfectionism on our mental health and relationships. Have you ever experienced anxiety or depression because of your pursuit of perfection? Have you ever pushed away loved ones because you were afraid to let them see your imperfections?

Finally, let's begin to uncover the ways in which we can break free from the mask of perfection. What are some things you can do today to embrace your true self, imperfections and all? Can you take a step back and acknowledge that you're human, that you make mistakes, and that it's okay?

Let's take a step towards embracing our true selves, imperfections and all. Let's break free from the mask of perfection and live a life that is authentic, raw, and real. We deserve it.

CHAPTER TWO

UNCOVERING OUR AUTHENTICITY

Uncovering Our Authenticity

It's time to uncover our true selves! Exploring our passions and values, identifying our strengths and weaknesses, and embracing our individuality.

For so long, we've been told to conform, to fit in, to be like everyone else. But what about our own unique voice, our own perspective, our own strengths and weaknesses?

It's time to break free from the mold of perfection and embrace our quirks and flaws. It's time to uncover our true selves and live a life that is authentic, raw, and real.

Some points to know uncover our Autheticity

- Exploring our passions and values
- Identifying our strengths and weaknesses
- Embracing our individuality
- Breaking free from the mold of perfection
- Uncovering our true selves

Reflection questions:

• What are your passions and values?

• What are your strengths and weaknesses?

• What makes you unique?

• How can you break free from the mold of perfection and embrace your quirks and flaws?

• What does your true self look like?

Let's take a step towards uncovering our true selves and living a life that is authentic, raw, and real.

Activity:

• Take a piece of paper and write down your passions and values.

• Draw a self-portrait that represents your true self.

• Write a letter to yourself embracing your quirks and flaws.

Let's embrace our individuality and live a life that is true to who we are!

CHAPTER THREE

THE BEAUTY OF IMPERMANENCE

The Beauty of Impermanence

Nature is imperfect, and that's what makes it beautiful. The impermanence of life and how it shapes us, letting go of the need for control, and finding beauty in the imperfect.

Some points to know the Beauty of Impermanence

- The impermanence of life and how it shapes us
- Letting go of the need for control
- Finding beauty in the imperfect

Reflection questions:

- How has impermanence shaped your life?
- What are some things you've tried to control, and how has that worked out for you?
- Where have you seen beauty in imperfection?

Activity:

- Take a walk outside and observe the imperfections in nature.
- Write a poem or journal entry about the beauty of impermanence.
- Create a piece of art that represents the beauty of

imperfection

Let's continue on this journey of self-discovery and embrace the beauty of impermanence.

CHAPTER FOUR

EMBRACING OUR SCARS

Embracing Our Scars

Our scars tell our story. Finding strength in our weaknesses, personal stories of resilience, and embracing our scars as part of our journey.

In this chapter, we'll explore:

• The power of vulnerability in sharing our scars
• Personal stories of resilience and strength
• Embracing our scars as part of our journey

Reflection questions:

• What are some scars you've been hiding or ashamed of?
• How have you found strength in your weaknesses?
• What's one scar you're willing to share with someone you trust?

Activity:

• Write a personal story of resilience and strength.
• Draw a self-portrait that includes your scars.
• Share a scar with someone you trust and receive support and validation.

Let's continue on this journey of self-discovery and embrace our scars.

CHAPTER FIVE

Breaking Free from Comparison

Breaking Free from Comparison

Comparison is the thief of joy. Recognizing the dangers of comparison, strategies for cultivating self-awareness, and embracing our unique journey.

In this chapter, we'll explore:

• The dangers of comparison

• Strategies for cultivating self-awareness

• Embracing our unique journey

Reflection questions:

• When do you find yourself comparing to others?

• How does comparison make you feel?

• What are some things you can do to cultivate self-awareness?

Activity:

• Write down three things you're grateful for about yourself.

- Take a social media detox for a day.
- Practice mindfulness meditation.

Let's break free from the comparison trap and embrace our unique journey.

Additional resources:

- "The Comparison Trap" by Sandra Flake
- "The Self-Awareness Workbook" by Dr. Tracy Packiam Alloway
- "Mindfulness: A Practical Guide to Finding Peace in a Frantic World" by Mark Williams and Danny Penman

Let's continue on this journey of self-discovery and break free from the comparison trap.

CHAPTER SIX

Vulnerability: The Power of Openness

Vulnerability: The Power of Openness

Vulnerability is strength, not weakness. Embracing vulnerability as a strength, building deeper connections through vulnerability, and practicing vulnerability in relationships.

In this chapter, we'll explore:

- The myth that vulnerability is weakness
- The power of vulnerability in building connections
- Practicing vulnerability in relationships

Reflection questions:

- When have you felt vulnerable in the past?
- How did it make you feel?
- What are some ways you can practice vulnerability in your relationships?

Activity:

- Write a letter to someone you trust, sharing your fears and insecurities.
- Practice active listening with a friend or loved one.
- Take a risk and share your true feelings with someone.

Let's embrace vulnerability as a strength and build deeper connections.

Additional resources:

- "The Gifts of Imperfection" by Brené Brown
- "Daring Greatly: How the Courage to Be Vulnerable Transforms the Way We Live, Love, Parent, and Lead" by Brené Brown
- "The Art of Vulnerability" by Teal Swan

Let's continue on this journey of self discovery and embrace vulnerability as a strength.

CHAPTER SEVEN

The Social Media Masquerade

The Social Media Masquerade

Social media is a highlight reel, but what's behind the curtain? The impact of social media on our self-esteem, tips for healthy social media habits, and embracing authenticity online.

In this chapter, we'll explore:

- The curated highlight reel of social media
- The impact on self-esteem and mental health
- Tips for healthy social media habits
- Embracing authenticity online

Reflection questions:

- How do you feel when you scroll through social media?
- What are some ways you can cultivate a healthy social media habit?
- How can you embrace authenticity online?

Activity:

- Take a social media detox for a day
- Post something authentic and vulnerable on social media
- Practice self-compassion when scrolling through social media

Let's break free from the social media masquerade and embrace authenticity online.

Additional resources:

- "The Social Media Upgrade" by Scott Steinberg
- "The Authenticity Hoax" by Andrew Potter
- "The Self-Esteem Workbook" by Glenn R. Schiraldi

Let's continue on this journey of self-discovery and break free from the social media masquerade.

CHAPTER EIGHT

SELF-ACCEPTANCE: THE PATH TO FREEDOM

Self-Acceptance: The Path to Freedom

Self-acceptance is the key to freedom. Practicing self-compassion and self-forgiveness, embracing our quirks and flaws, and letting go of the need for perfection.

In this chapter, we'll explore:

- The importance of self-acceptance
- Practicing self-compassion and self-forgiveness
- Embracing our quirks and flaws
- Letting go of the need for perfection

Reflection questions:

- What are some things you've been too hard on yourself about?
- How have you practiced self-compassion in the past?
- What are some quirks and flaws you're willing to embrace?

Activity:

- Write a self-compassion letter to yourself.
- Practice self-forgiveness and let go of a past mistake.
- Create a self-acceptance mantra and repeat it daily.

Let's embrace self-acceptance and walk the path to freedom.

Additional resources:

- "The Self-Acceptance Workbook" by Dr. Tracy Packiam Alloway
- "The Gifts of Imperfection" by Brené Brown
- "The Power of Now" by Eckhart Tolle

Let's continue on this journey of self-discovery and embrace self-acceptance.

CHAPTER NINE

CONCLUSION - INTEGRATING THE JOURNEY

Conclusion - Integrating the Journey

In this final chapter, we'll integrate the key takeaways from our journey together, celebrating your growth and progress. We'll also explore ways to continue nurturing your self-awareness, self-acceptance, and self-expression.

Topics:

- Reflecting on your journey and progress
- Integrating insights and lessons learned
- Embracing your authentic self
- Continuing education and self-reflection
- Sharing your light with others

Reflection questions:

- What are some key insights or lessons you've learned on your journey?
- How have you grown or changed in ways you didn't expect?

• What are some areas where you'd like to continue learning or growing?

Activity:

• Write a personal manifesto or creed
• Create a self-care and self-reflection plan
• Develop a strategy to share your insights and experiences with others

By integrating the journey, you can:

• Embody your authentic self with confidence
• Continue growing and learning with intention
• Share your light and inspire others
• Stay true to your path and trust your inner guidance

Congratulations on completing our journey together! Remember, self-discovery and self-acceptance are lifelong paths. Stay curious, stay open, and keep shining your light!

CHAPTER TEN

The New Beginning - Embracing Your True Self

The New Beginning - Embracing Your True Self

In this final chapter, we celebrate your journey and welcome the new beginning that awaits you. You've worked tirelessly to discover and accept your true self, and now it's time to embrace and live as your authentic self.

Topics:

• Celebrating your journey and progress
• Embracing your true self and all its aspects
• Trusting yourself and your inner guidance
• Living authentically and unapologetically
• Sharing your light and inspiring others

Reflection questions:

• What are some key takeaways from your journey?
• How has your self-awareness and self-acceptance

evolved?

• What does living authentically mean to you?

Activity:

• Write a letter to yourself, celebrating your growth and progress

• Create a self-love and self-care plan to support your new beginning

• Develop a plan to share your light and inspire others

By embracing your true self, you can:

• Live a life that is authentic, meaningful, and fulfilling

• Trust yourself and your inner guidance

• Share your gifts and talents with the world

• Inspire others with your confidence and self-love

Congratulations, dear friend! You've reached the end of our journey together, but this is just the beginning of your new life as your true self. Go forth and shine your light!

Final Message :embracing The Journey Ahead

Embracing the Journey Ahead

As we come to the end of this book, remember that your journey of self-discovery and self-acceptance is ongoing. This chapter offers final thoughts and encouragement as you continue on your path.

Topics:

- Embracing the ups and downs of life's journey
- Trusting yourself and your inner guidance
- Cultivating gratitude and appreciation
- Staying present and mindful in the moment
- Embracing the mystery and uncertainty of life

Reflection questions:

- What have you learned about yourself and your journey so far?
- How have you grown or changed in ways you didn't expect?
- What are some things you're looking forward to exploring or experiencing in the future?

Activity:

- Write a letter to yourself to be read in 6-12 months
- Create a vision board or collage representing your future goals and aspirations
- Develop a daily or weekly practice to stay present and mindful

By embracing the journey ahead, you can:

- Stay curious and open to new experiences and learning
- Trust yourself and your inner guidance
- Find joy and gratitude in the present moment

• Embrace the unknown with confidence and courage

Remember, your journey is unique and ongoing. Stay true to yourself, trust your path, and keep shining your light!

A Poem To Motivate You :)

Born to be real, not perfect

Embracing flaws, our true self respect
Unique and quirky, we stand tall
Authenticity shines, perfection falls

Be you, brave and true
No mask needed, just you
Celebrate individuality
Embrace your realness, wild and free.

A POEM TO MOTIVATE YOU :)

A POEM TO MOTIVATE YOU :)

A POEM TO MOTIVATE YOU :)